Breakfast With Jesus

Ivan King

All situations and events depicted are from the author's perspective and perception. No harm is intended to any person, alive or dead, whom the author knows or has known.

The author reserves all rights. Except for literary reviews, any use of this material, whole or in part, or, referenced in any way by any medium including, but not limited to: electronic, mechanical, or digital copy; and any recording thereof (Auditory, Digital, or Written) is forbidden without prior written permission from the author.

Breakfast With Jesus

Author: Ivan King
Printed by: Valley Group Media, LLC.
Editing: David T. Williams
Cover Art: Tyler D. Masterson
ISBN-13: 978-1514353349
Copyright: Ivan King / Valley Group Media, LLC.
First Printing: January 25, 2015 United States of America
Copyright © 2015 Ivan King
All rights reserved.

Table of Contents

Hear What the Critics are Saying

Editorial Review

About the Book

Breakfast With Jesus

Excerpt From Another Book

Ivan King Library

Meet the Author

Hear What the Critics are Saying

"Very inspirational and powerful; everyone should read this book. **Breakfast With Jesus** is by far one of the best Christian books to have come out in the last decade."

-Mary Jones -Valley Daily News

"I give this book **Five Stars All The Way!** This book makes my list as one of the top reads in the Christian genre. Anyone of Faith will enjoy this book very much."

-Theresa Davis –Alliance Media Group

"**Breakfast With Jesus** was a very powerful and thought provoking book. Every generation, young and old, should have to read this book. **Ten Thumbs Up.**"

-Dave Baker -Book Bloggers of America

"This was an excellent book; it was short, I ended up reading it in less than two hours; however, it has a very strong and positive message. **A Must Read."**

-Lisa Cooper -Literary Times Inc.

"This was a very powerful book. It had a very solid message about love and forgiveness. **Highly Recommend."**

-Emma Righter -Writers United Group

"**Amazing book!** I fell to my knees at the end and cried. This book reminded me why I became a born-again Christian. Its messages are not only powerful, but also true."

-Carl Mosner –Readers Cove Unlimited

"A friend from work recommended this book to me and although I am not a Christian, I was still moved by its **Powerful Message."**

-Lee Ratner –Daily Media Trends, Inc.

Editorial Review

Breakfast With Jesus is a very spiritual and powerful book. Its messages are time tested and true. This book really made me think, but more importantly, it made me feel.

If you are looking for a book that will move you to tears, then look no further than **Breakfast With Jesus;** a masterful book that will not only inspire you to become a better person, but it will also teach you some of life's greatest lessons. **Inspirational Book!**

David T. Williams

About the Book

A young man has breakfast with Jesus and discovers the meaning of life. What lessons will he learn? What secrets are going to be revealed?

Jump into this inspiring book and you will find out.....

If you could have a private conversation with Jesus Christ and ask him anything you wanted, what would ask him?

"I am the Way, the Truth, and the Life. No one comes to the Father except through me."

Jesus Christ

Breakfast With Jesus

My day started out like any other day. I was in the kitchen preparing breakfast, before going to work; cream cheese spread over rye toast and coffee. The breakfast of champions! As usual, I was running late, and it certainly didn't help my cause any when I spilled cream cheese all over my new silk tie.

"This is how my day is going to start," I said to myself after letting out a long drawn sigh. I rushed quickly to the sink; lowering my tie into the basin, I tried desperately to wash it out before it stained.

Just as I was vigorously cleaning my tie, and cursing under my breath, it happened…..Jesus Christ walked into my kitchen.

"Hello, Michael," he said with the most beautiful and peaceful smile I have ever seen. "I am Jesus."

Out of total shock, I jumped up immediately and yelled. "Sir, I don't know who you are and how you got in here. But you need to get out of my house now!" I reached desperately for the frying pan and held it firm in my right hand. I held it out in front while making a real threatening swinging motion to let him know I meant business.

"You know exactly who I am," he said with such a smooth voice. He seemed sincere and very humble; he was almost childlike. "Because I just told you."

"Look," I said angrily while holding the frying pan out in front with both hands, grasping tightly around the handle as though it were a tennis racket. "I'm warning you; if you don't get out of here, I'm calling the cops!"

"Are you sure you want to that? Because I'm only here to help you," he said with an extremely relaxing tone of voice. He had a very serene look; like twin wells of purity, his eyes reflected gentleness and compassion.

"Help me," I snorted sarcastically. "Who says I need any help!"

"Michael, you are a man who has lost his

ways and I am here to put you back on the right path," he said with a brutally honest stare.

"Look, just drop the act, I know that you are not Jesus and if you leave now, I promise you that I won't call the cops," but even as I said that, I let my guard down just a bit; truth was, this man was very non-threatening. He was the opposite of aggressive.

"How do you know for certain that I am not who I say I am?" He asked.

"Well, for starters, you are way too short to be Jesus; second of all, Jesus had long hair and lastly, Jesus died over two thousand years ago; so you see, there's no way that you can be him." I responded in a calm and matter-of-fact manner.

"I am not too short! I am exactly as my Father has made me." Jesus said in a very passionate tone.

I had finally had enough; so I decided to take a different approach, turning towards him I said, "Okay, if you really are who you say you are, then prove it."

"I have no need to prove myself to you," he said abruptly.

"Yeah, but do you have any idea how many people in the world claim to be you? Not eight blocks from here there is a mental hospital full of crazies claiming to be Jesus! What makes you any different from them?"

"I am different from them because I am the one True Son of God."

"Ok, then let me ask you this, what's the winning numbers to this weekend's Powerball?" I asked him with a smirk on my face.

"I am the Son of Man; not your personal genie," he responded with an amicable grin. He also had an amazing level of patience and calmness in his voice.

"Well, I remember that in Sunday school, they taught us about all the wonderful miracles you performed back in those days. But isn't that how people knew that you were the Son of God; didn't you have to walk on water and raise the dead in order for them to believe?"

"Those with pure hearts do not need to be swayed. A man with a clean conscious and a clear line of sight will surely see the truth; especially when it's right in front of his very eyes."

"Okay," I said finally caving in. I put the frying pan into the sink and said, "Let's say, just for argument's sake, that you are Jesus. Then what are you doing here; why are you in my kitchen?"

"That's easy," he said with a friendly and inviting smile. "I am here to have breakfast with you."

My house sits all alone, at an abandoned cul-de-sac, in a forgotten part of the world. But on this day, I sat in my kitchen and had breakfast with Jesus.

"I don't really have anything to offer as far as a decent breakfast," I said feeling kind of down on myself for not having a nice spread to put out.

"What about all the wonderful things you have just sitting on the counter?" Jesus asked, pointing for me to turn around.

When I did, I couldn't believe my eyes! On top of the counter there was an entire tray full of yummy breakfast treats. There were fruits and a bevy of pastries. There was even a pitcher of juice, and yet another filled with coffee.

Unable to divert my eyes, I was stunned into submission. The realization of what was truly happening was too much to bear. I took a seat at the table just so I wouldn't pass out.

"So you really are Jesus!" I said pointing to him with wide eyes of disbelief.

"That is exactly what I have been telling you all along," he said playfully, and then Jesus got up and poured himself a cup of coffee. He took a long, hard sip as he closed his eyes and said, "Oh, there is nothing quite like a cup of joe in the morning!"

"You drink coffee?" I asked in amazement.

Upon hearing that, Jesus let out a strong belly laugh. It wasn't a very usual laugh; it felt more profound, like the type that comes from deep within a man's soul. I suddenly found myself laughing right along with him.

"Of course I drink coffee," he said bluntly. "Doesn't everybody?"

"Wow," I said under my breath, while still trying desperately to wrap my head around the fact that Jesus was in my house; he was in kitchen! "So why are you here?" I asked.

"I told you," he said with a wide open and honest smile. "I'm here to have breakfast with you."

"Yes, but why me?"

"Because Michael, you have a big hole, deep inside of you, and I want to shine some light into that darkness."

"Yeah I got that," I said timidly. "But shouldn't you be on CNN, or standing on top of a mountain someplace where the entire world can see you?"

"I win the world over one soul at a time. Michael, if I can bring just a single person back into my Father's house, then I will have gained something more precious than the entire world put together."

What Jesus said really made me think. For a long time I had been feeling hollow and empty. Truth was, I stood on the edge of an emotional abyss and didn't quite know how to work my way back; I felt alone now, lost in a heartless world where not a single person cares about your troubles. In my attempts to fill that emptiness, I reached out for whatever I could find, but nothing would quell that void deep inside.

After getting his coffee, Jesus came back to the table and sat across from me. Following a couple moments of silence, I got up and poured myself a cup as well; then, I sat back down and reflected quietly. I was staring at Jesus; I was looking right into the eyes of the Son of God; I had so many questions.

Finally, after working up the courage, I said to him, "I have lots of questions."

"I have all the answers; I am the Truth," he responded.

I thought very hard and very long about what I would ask him first. After taking another long sip I turned to Jesus and fired off my first question, "What is the meaning of life?"

"Life does not have one singular meaning because it is full of purpose. There are many things we must accomplish before it is all said and done."

"That's not exactly the answer I was looking for," I said rather glumly.

"Ah," said Jesus holding up a finger and jumping up excitedly from his chair. "However,

I can tell you the two most important reasons."

I was suddenly intrigued by what he had to say; I sat up in my chair. "I'm all ears," I said enthusiastically.

"The meaning of life is to love and forgive," he said plainly.

"To Love and Forgive?" I asked, "Why is that more important than everything else."

"People earn their way into my Father's house; they do so by loving one another and forgiving each other. You have to love hard; even when the person does not love you back. You have to love others just as much as you love yourself; and above it all, you have to love my Father for the mercy he has bestowed upon you."

"Wait, you are saying I have to love people even when they hurt me; or steal from me, or do me harm?"

"Especially then."

"Why especially then?" I asked.

"Because, love and sacrifice are forever linked to one another; it is easy to love when things are going well and not so easy when you hurt inside. But it is precisely during those tough moments when you find out the true nature of the person you really are."

"So I have to love those around me no matter what?" I asked, somewhat skeptical.

"Yes, because love shines light into even the darkest corners of a man's soul; more importantly, without a pure heart, one that truly knows how to love, you will never bask in my Father's glory."

"Okay," I said but then asked, "Why is forgiveness so important?"

"Michael, I want you to pay very close attention to what I am about to say," he said. Then he paused to look at me in order to make sure I was listening. "You have to forgive the people who have wronged you; and you always have to ask the Father for forgiveness from your mistakes."

"But why is that so important?"

"Because, a heart which does not forgive can never be forgiven," he said with a very serious expression on his face.

"Wait, so if someone kills a person I love, I

have to forgive them for it?" I had to ask because just the mere thought sounded ludicrous to me.

"Yes, because it is not your place to judge or to cast blame. Only the Father can do that; you have to trust in him. You must have faith in his process and know that what he is doing is for the greater good."

"Okay," I said with a little extra pep in my voice. "That brings us to my following question; why does God let bad things happen to good people? I mean, how could he allow so many people to die at Auschwitz, or during the Twin Towers attacks on 911? Why does God sit idly by and let these horrible things happen?"

Jesus stood up and began pacing back and forth. After a long moment of being lost in a maze of his own thoughts, he turned to me and said, "A long time ago, my Father built a house. It was the most magnificent thing he ever created. Now, upon building this beautiful house, he wanted to share it with somebody; so he invited some guests to stay in the house. These guests were his family, and he explained to them that, while staying at his house, they could do whatever they pleased; however, my

Father had one rule, and one rule only. There was a room in the house where these guests could not go. One day, my father left his guests to their own devices, and when he came back, he was shocked to learn they had disobeyed his only command. When this happened, my Father did not get angry; he became disappointed, which is something way worse than anger." He stopped momentarily to look at me and asked, "Michael, do you know what my Father did with these guests?"

"I imagine he kicked them out of his house," I immediately responded.

"Not exactly, for you see, my Father is too merciful to leave his children out in the cold. But also, my Father did not want to be known as a tyrant, forcing his guests to live under his rules. He just wanted them to be happy and enjoy life. As a result, he gave them the gift of freedom; the gift of choice."

"I don't understand," I said feeling confused. "What does any of this have to do with bad things happening to good people?" I asked.

"Because, cause and effect are a byproduct

of the choices we make."

"I don't follow you," I said feeling even more confused than ever.

Jesus looked deep into my eyes with a piercing gaze and said, "I know that more than anything you just want to be happy, but the fruition of your dreams will forever be limited by the choices you make. Michael, choices in and out of themselves are neither good nor bad; however, it is their corrosive intentions that define them. What I am saying to you is that, good or bad, God cannot make your choices for you; therefore, you must make your own choices in life. Whatever choices you make, and how you decide to live your life afterwards, is what is going to determine its value."

"Are you saying then, that those good people chose to have bad things happen to them?" I asked, feeling befuddled by the complexity of it all.

Jesus explained his point even further by adding, "Freedom of choice was given to you; and what you decide to do with it is entirely up to you. If someone makes a bad choice, an evil choice, like let's say, fly a plane into a building and murder thousands of people, they are exercising their God given right to choose. But one day, every person alive and dead will stand before the Father and take responsibility for the choices they have made."

"Hold on, are you saying that God has no control over any of this Chaos?" I asked sitting up in my chair and crossing my arms.

"To the contrary, everything that has happened, and that ever will happen, only does so because it is the wish of the Father. God, in his infinite wisdom gave you the gift of choice, but it is called upon you to use that gift wisely," he said.

I paused and let the idea swim around my head for a bit. What Jesus said made me reflect on my own life; my own choices. I realized that sometimes, there is a big difference between the person we are and the person we wish we were. For me, that difference is as wide as the sea and twice as deep. I have never been one to believe that the things which happened to us in the past, good or bad, have a profound impact on the ways in which we live our lives. I always thought to the contrary, now I'm not so sure. "You are saying then that we were given the freedom of choice by God; but some people choose to do bad things with that freedom?"

"Yes," responded Jesus.

"But God won't intervene in the choices we make; good or bad, he lets us decide the path we take?" I asked.

"Exactly," said Jesus excitedly, flying out of his chair once more. "Remember when I said earlier that sooner or later everyone must stand before the Father and account for the choices they have made?"

"Yes," I responded shaking my head from side to side.

"Well in the end, the intensity of your escape will not matter; whether your displacement is mental, emotional or physical, eventually you will come face to face with the self realization that the roots of your sins originate in the past pulling at you through time, like taught rubber bands."

My mind was racing a mile a minute. My breathing became sporadic and I could hear the constant pounding of my beating heart. Suddenly, I had a moment of insight and said, "You are saying that God does not allow bad things to happen to good people; he does however, allow people to choose, and sometimes people make evil choices that affect good people."

"You are beginning to understand," Jesus said with a hopeful smile, only now he was even more animated than before as he moved his hands about wildly.

A thought occurred to me, so I turned to Jesus and said, "What about the Big Bang? There has been so much that science has proven, which goes against the teachings of the bible. I mean, how do you explain things like evolution for example?"

"Nothing that science has done so far disproves the existence of God," he said.

"Yeah but there is so much evidence now that is contrary to what the bible says."

"Michael, God created man and woman in Adam and Eve; he also imbedded within their matrix the ability to evolve. God has made all of this possible. Remember, he made man in his own image. Therefore, God created mankind so that they may think for themselves and grow."

"But how do you explain the theory of the

Big Bang?" I asked.

"At the very instant in which God said: Let there be light. That was the immaculate birth of creation and the Big Bang was the moment of this conception. However, it did not happen by some random chain of events; the beginning of all things was created by God."

"But the Big Bang happened billions of years ago," I added. "Yet, all of the events in the bible take place only a few thousand years ago."

"The concept of time was created by mankind; outside of this reality it does not exist. There is no way to quantify a day of God's time, because it does not exist. In our reality there is no moon; there is no sun. In heaven, not only is life eternal but so is time."

"What's it like to live in heaven?" I asked with childlike wonder.

"Heaven is whatever you want it to be; in heaven you will always find what you are looking for."

"Do you guys have TVs in heaven?" I asked with a serious look, sprinkled with a soft smile. "Do you get cable in heaven?"

Jesus let out a strong laugh. He laughed so hard, tears began to run down his rosy cheeks.

"What's so funny?" I asked.

"No Michael, we do not have TVs in heaven."

"No HBO?" I asked with an innocent stare. "I just can't imagine living in a place for all eternity and not being able to find out how Game of Thrones ends."

"It ends with Daenerys Targaryen becoming the queen of the entire world only then to be eaten by her own dragons."

"Hello?" I said waving my arms to Jesus.

"What?" He asked, with an almost innocent stare.

"Spoiler alert!" I complained vehemently.

"At least now you won't be needing that TV you love so much."

"I guess not." I said reluctantly, but added, "I'll just come and find you whenever I want to know how one of my shows ended."

"Fair enough," he said, letting out a short laugh.

"How do you know these things if you are not present all the time?" I asked intuitively.

"But I am always present," he said abruptly.

"I have never seen you before."

"There is a part of me that lives within every person on this planet. He is the messenger; the one that will stand before the Almighty on your behalf."

"Like a lawyer you mean?"

"No, not really, he is more of a counselor than a lawyer."

"So through me this counselor sees everything that I see?" I asked.

"Exactly, he bears witness to everything you experience in life; all that you know, the counselor within you also knows. Therefore, I know and so does my Father."

"Hold on a second, you mean to tell me all of those days I spent alone in my bedroom as a teenager, discovering how my body works and learning how to become a man, you know about that?"

"Everything you do is witnessed by the

counselor; good or bad, we have seen all that you have done," he said giving me a stern look.

"Wow, that's scary!" I blurted out.

"That's why you have to pay close attention and choose your path wisely. Because everything you do has a consequence to be paid."

"Wait," I said with a sudden sense of concern. "What if I make mistakes along the way?"

"You simply fall down. But falling is integral part of the process, because it is how we learn and become stronger. However, you must admit your mistakes to God and ask him for forgiveness from your misdeeds."

"Right," I said pointing to Jesus excitedly. "And God will only forgive me if, in turn I have forgiven others."

"Yes, this is true," Jesus said.

"Okay, so I get how people have the freedom to make their own choices; and that sometimes they choose to do evil things to each other, but that still does not explain natural disasters?"

"What do you mean?" He asked me with a smooth and gentle voice.

"Like the tsunami of 2004 in Indonesia. A quarter of a million people died for absolutely no reason. How could God have allowed that to happen?"

"This planet is no different than you and I. It too has a mind and a life of its own. The earth must go through its own growing pains. Remember what I said about cause and effect? If God should control what happens to the planet, by default he would also be controlling what happens to you; therefore, altering your freedom of choice. When a volcano erupts, that is the planet doing what the planet wants to do. But all of these things are a consequence of the original sin."

"The original sin?" I asked, feeling somewhat bewildered.

"You mention the bible a lot but you don't actually know what's said in there, do you?" Jesus asked, in a scolding tone of voice.

"No I don't," I admitted candidly. "I know more about the bible from reading The Da Vinci Code, than I do from actually reading the bible?"

"Ha," Jesus said and snorted rather loudly. "That is one trashy piece of literature if ever there was one?"

"So you know about that too?" I asked.

"Of course, I told you, through the counselor we know everything that happens on this planet."

"Since we are on the subject," I spouted out clumsily. "Did you get married to Mary Magdalene?"

Jesus stood up again and walked around pensively; then he turned to me and said, "It is true that I loved her more than I loved my other disciples, but not in the kind of way that a man loves a woman."

"In what kind of way did you love her?" I asked with a genuine interest.

"In the same type of way in which a father loves his sons and daughters."

"Do you believe in equality between men and women?" I asked.

"The concept of inequality was created by

mankind, not by God. It is another one of the many bad fruits from man's tree of choices."

"Earlier you said that I have darkness within me," I said with a burning curiosity.

"Yes,"

"What does that mean?" I asked.

"It means that you feel alone; that you have lost hope."

"Hope?" I asked furrowing my brow. "What exactly do you mean by that?"

"Hope is a tender whisper in the wind that keeps dreams alive. It is the reason we get up every morning and struggle to make a better life for ourselves and for the people we care about. It's what keeps you going after suffering through so much pain and sorrow."

"How do I find this hope?" I asked.

"You don't have to look for it because it's still inside of you; only it has dug itself down deep."

"Can it be lost forever?"

"Definitely," responded Jesus without even thinking about it.

"How?" I asked.

"The absolute absence of hope only happens when you lose the ability to be forgiven."

"How do I lose the ability to be forgiven?"

"By dying," he said bluntly.

"You're saying that once I die I can no longer be forgiven for the bad choices I have made?"

"Precisely," he said.

"Wow, you weren't kidding when you spoke about the importance of forgiveness!"

"I was absolutely not kidding! There is nothing more serious and sacred to me than for you to know everlasting life."

"I was always taught that you get into heaven by being a good person," I said with an optimistic smile.

"You were taught wrong," Jesus said plainly.

"How does one get into heaven?" I asked.

"By understanding and accepting that I have already paid the price for the poor choices you have made. But also, you have to forgive and ask for forgiveness; and finally, you must have a pure heart."

"Wait, when did you pay the price for my poor choices?" I asked, looking up at him.

"I died on the cross so you wouldn't have to. If you believe in my blood and my sacrifice, I promise you that you will know the True Face of God. But no one comes to the Father except through me."

"What if I don't accept; what if I don't believe?" I asked with a bit of defiance in my voice.

"Then you will never know the light of life; you will forever walk in darkness," Jesus said.

"That sounds horrible! Just thinking about it makes my chest hurt all over."

After pacing a bit more, Jesus sat back down and got suddenly very serious. He looked at me with sad and caring eyes. I could tell he wanted to tell me something, but didn't quite know how.

"Michael, I don't ever want for you to go to that place?"

We sat quietly for several minutes; each lost in our own minds. I took another long sip from my coffee cup and Jesus took one from his.

After a long, almost awkward silence I asked, "This place you are talking about, is it hell?"

"Yes," he said with a frown, and a heavy sigh.

"What is hell like?" I asked with wanton curiosity.

"It's a place of unimaginable horrors," he said with dark, solemn eyes.

"Could you take me there and show me?"

"Yes, but if I did," he said with a smoldering look, and a very somber tone of voice. "If I were to take you to hell for only one minute; the pain and agony that you would experience in just that one minute would be enough to drive you completely insane."

"But only bad people go to hell right?" I asked sounding anxious, and worried.

"Hell is full of good people," said Jesus.

"But why?" I asked with a deeply sad and distraught voice. "Why do good people go to hell?"

"You only have the ability see what a man can do; therefore, the good and the bad become quickly visible. But God can see into a man's heart."

"I thought being good automatically meant that you have a good heart," I said, almost pleading.

"Not necessarily, many people do good things all while having poisoned hearts. Michael, from the very moment in which you were brought into this world, you were born with an impure heart. In God's eyes, everyone is unclean; every heart is impure and, unless they change, will forever fall short of his glory."

"How can you be born with an impure heart?" I asked, feeling a bit lost and confused. "How can a baby be considered unclean?"

"It all goes back to when Adam and Eve originally sinned against God; the result of that sin is infused into the very foundation of who you are. Sin is an inescapable reality; everyone who lives has sinned against God."

"Wait," I said with nervous enthusiasm. "Are you telling me that I am paying the price for the sins committed by two people whom I have never met?"

"No you are not," he said firmly.

"But you just said that I have sinned from the day I was born?"

"Yes, but that is the reason why the Father sent me to the cross; so that I may cleanse you of this sin. Michael, I bore that heavy burden for you. All you have to do is have faith in me and believe that I died for you. I promise you, if you ask God for forgiveness, you will be forgiven and absolved of your sins."

"Wow, this is all so shocking," I said looking up at the ceiling and scratching my head in wonder. "I never thought it was possible for good people to end up in hell."

"Yes," he said and added, "Hell is a very real and scary place; and if you don't repent from your sins, you will end up going there."

"Are people like Hitler and Stalin in hell?"

"Yes," he said.

"They're all there together?" I asked, "The good people, mixed in with the bad ones?"

"Everyone who does not follow God's commandments will end up in the same place."

"Is Michael Jackson in Hell?"

"Yes," Jesus replied succinctly.

"But why, he was beloved by so many people?"

"Because he chose to ignore God's laws and made all of the wrong choices."

Shaking my head and feeling overwhelmed by the weight of what Jesus was saying, I turned to him and asked, "How long do I have?"

"How long do you have for what?" He asked.

"How long do I have to live, before I die?"

"Only God knows that answer," he said, but also added, "I can tell you this, you should live every moment like it's your very last. Because once you die, all that you have done will be put on a scale."

"What should I do next?"

"You have to accept me into your heart, and repent from your sins; then you have to ask the Father for forgiveness so that you may be spiritually born-again."

"What words should I say?" I asked.

"The words you choose are not important; the only thing that matters is the genuine intent of your heart."

Suddenly, I was flooded by a tsunami of emotions. Fighting them back was like trying to contain a storm in a glass of water. Tears began to run down my face. I dropped to my knees in front of Jesus and cried uncontrollably; clinging to him, I closed my eyes and said, "Jesus, please accept me into your heart and help me heal this pain. Forgive me for all of the ways in which I have wronged against God. Jesus I want to be reborn; I want to be made whole again. I want to walk with you in the light and never know that place of darkness."

After what seemed like an eternity, Jesus lifted me up by my arms and gave me a hug. He wiped away my tears and smiled; when he did, his smile somehow shone light into my personal darkness, illuminating the path I was on. It gave me strength.

Jesus gave me hope.

Then he simply said his goodbyes and began to leave. As Jesus walked away, he turned to me for the last time and said, "Michael, the freedom of choice is the greatest gift you will ever have, and how you use it will determine its value."

The End

Breakfast With Jesus

"I am the light of the world. Whoever follows me will never walk in darkness, but will have the light of life."

Jesus Christ

*****

Dear Friend,

If you would like to do your part to spread the word about this wonderful book; please post it to your **Facebook** wall, and tell at least ten of your closest friends about its powerful message.

Forever Grateful,

Ivan King

Breakfast With Jesus

In This Book, and my other book <u>Hell: A Place Without Hope,</u> I share this message of Salvation with you in the hopes that someday you will learn the truth about God's glorious plan for your life. Turn to Christ and confess your sins; only then, will you find true happiness and everlasting life.

Breakfast With Jesus

Breakfast With Jesus

Ivan King

Breakfast With Jesus

Excerpt From Another Book

Hell: A Place Without Hope
Ivan King

Gabriel watched over them. Even though they did not believe in his existence; it made no difference to him, because he believed in them. More importantly, he still held on to hope. But now, it was apparent to him that the 'lost' (that's how he referred to them) needed him more than ever before. He was not all knowing, like the Almighty One; but this he knew for sure, because he could see it in their demeanor and sense it in their despair. They were lost; fallen victims of an implacable and cruel world. Pity welt up within Gabriel's being. Just looking at them saddened him deeply; he wanted to reach out, to help in some way, but didn't exactly know how.

But now, even as a thousand years had passed, he is keenly aware of the dangers ahead. He eternally stands guard, caring for and watching over his battleground labyrinth. He is determined that not a soul shall be lost…not on his watch. Despite the fact that the maze of interconnecting caves he guards over is dark, he knows its twists and turns all too well. He is familiar with every inch of the ground he so proudly protects. And although the eternally lit candles attached to the rocky walls only gives off enough light to see a foot or so around it, he is well aware of the darkness that lies in wait.

The walls of the caves were wide enough where an average sized person could stand out his or her arms and touch both sides. But the height of it could not be reached even if two men stood on each other's shoulders.

Suddenly, Gabriel heard soft whimpers coming from the far corner of a pathway leading to the north end of the labyrinth. Making haste, he made his way over there so fast it almost seemed as though he were gliding. He quickly passed through many shadowy pockets of darkness, spreading out into the far reaches of the unknown. He had an instinct for his surroundings; but, a bat-like sense of sonar is what really guided him to the noise.

When he reached the soft but steady whimper, he saw another lost. He was at the far end of the cave with his back towards Gabriel. He was all alone, sitting in a dark corner, crying. Feeling that time was of the utmost importance, he leaped across the shadows and knelt beside one of God's lost children.

Download Today on Amazon.com

Hell: A Place Without Hope
Ivan King

Breakfast With Jesus

Ivan King Library

The Path

Angel Wars

Breakfast With Jesus

Hell: A Place Without Hope

The Dark Room

Who Ate My Grapes?

The Blue Gumball

Good Things Take Time

You Can Do It!

Old Man Hollow

Breakfast With Jesus

Meet the Author

Ivan King is an Award Winning and Best Selling Author of over 20 books. His #1 Book on Amazon, Breakfast With Jesus, has become a major success internationally. Mr. King was born in Rio de Janeiro, Brazil, in 1977, though his stay in Rio was to be short lived. Adopted from an orphanage, he was raised in Ipatinga's, Valley of Steel. His favorite author is Hemingway; yet his favorite book, is Steinbeck's Grapes of Wrath. When he is not writing or reading, he plays chess and the guitar.

When Ivan was eight, he read his first book, Judy Blume's Superfudge and the rest is history. That's the story behind how the passion for reading began; how it ends...has yet to be written.

Currently, he is working on a couple dozen writing projects and turning some of his novels into screenplays. Ivan's first published work, The Dark Room, is a Fiction Novel loosely based on his life growing up in the favelas, or slums, of Brazil.

Favorite quote: "In life, incredible things happen and unforgettable moments do exist; but nothing compares to having been loved by you, and though you rest in peace, I will miss and love you always."

If you would like to learn more about Ivan King, you can send him a message at:

WWW.IVANKING.COM

Printed in the USA
CPSIA information can be obtained
at www.ICGtesting.com
LVHW041016260424
778539LV00021B/141